snakes

& babies

poems
by Jules Gibbs

snakes

& babies

poems
by Jules Gibbs

The Sheep Meadow Press
Rhinebeck, New York

Designed and typeset by The Sheep Meadow Press
Distributed by Syracuse University Press

Cover Image: Alesso Baldovinetti, *Madonna and Child*

Library of Congress Cataloging-in-Publication-Data

Names: Gibbs, Jules, author.
Title: Snakes & babies : poems / by Jules Gibbs.
Description: Rhinebeck, New York : The Sheep Meadow Press, 2020.
Identifiers: LCCN 2020046822 | ISBN 9781937679897 (paperback)
Subjects: LCGFT: Poetry.
Classification: LCC PS3607.I2256 S63 2021 | DDC 811/.6--dc23
LC record available at https://lccn.loc.gov/2020046822

Published by
Sheep Meadow Press
P.O Box 84
Rhinebeck, NY 12572

for Bruce

ACKNOWLEDGMENTS

Some of the conceptual material in the series of poems "Snake" and "Baby" is informed by Sigmund Freud's *The Interpretation of Dreams*. The poem "Stay" concludes with "spirit ditties of no tone," which is a phrase taken from Keats' "Ode on a Grecian Urn." The idea of "entering from the dream side," in "Notes," is borrowed with grateful acknowledgment from Anne Carson's essay, "Every Exit is an Entrance (A Praise of Sleep)."

Many thanks to the editors of these journals for publishing the following poems, often in different forms and under different titles:

Ambit Magazine (London): "Thin"; *Spoon River Poetry Review*: "Wants," "Drift," "Blow," "Target"; Forklift, Ohio: "Joke," "Pin," "X"; *The Antioch Review*: "In oyster piles you saw their boots…," "The women are complaining…," "I love hate the beauty here…"; *Plume Poetry*: "Cave," "Fold," "The furniture breaks," "When the bear finally arrives"; *Plume Anthology 8*: "She would kill something"; *The American Poetry Journal*: "Crash"; H_NGM_N: "Bind"; *The Comstock Review*: "Wing"; *Better Magazine*: "Fin"; *NightBlock* "A bud plus a droplet," "There is an eye that is everywhere," "A lightening strike cracked," "Here you think in mist," "Rain through borders," "The bay at the end of the road," "Sickness of wet"; Bear Review: "She," "Keep"; *Dream Pop Press*: "bacteria scribble the chest…", "blood fur or is it snow chatter…"; *Figure 1*: "you could go to church with your mom…", "the dog's head splits, each neck a plume…"; *Salt Hill Journal*: "Drive," "Stay." Poems from the section, "Snake," were published in the anthology, *Gods & Monsters*, by *The American Poetry Journal*.

I would like to thank my colleagues, students, and fellow union members at Syracuse University for the privilege of learning from you and working by your side in the pursuit of art and justice. For the sustenance provided by an inclusive arts community, my thanks to Tere Paniagua and the Punto de Contacto family.

To Sheila Gulley Pleasants and all the good people at Virginia Center for Creative Arts, and to Cyndy Hayward at Willapa Bay Artist-in-Residence, for residencies where much of this book took shape — thank you for periodically rescuing me from the jaws of the domestic.

To fellow poets and artists who have offered crucial support — I cannot name everyone, but I must thank by name Louis S. Asekoff, Peter Balakian, Rachel Eliza Griffiths, Sarah Harwell, Stanley Moss, Kevin O'Connell, Ira Sadoff, and Jane Springer.

A debt of gratitude is owed to Matt Hart, who read this manuscript from its very early stages, and upon whom I have relied for feedback, some necessary distortion, and big-hearted amplification.

Thank you to my family, editors-at-large, for your support: to my mother, Ellen, my stepfather, Joe, and my siblings Caroline, Joe, and Connor.

Finally, Bruce, who feeds body and poem: for your generous brilliance (measured and mystical), for the space and the faith and the dog and the pizza (fig and pig) to do this — you put the Vitamin L (love) in all of it, and this book is for you.

CONTENTS

Blicke umher:
sieh, wie's lebendig wird rings —
Beim Tode! Lebendig!
Wahr spricht, wer Schatten spricht.

Look around:
look how it all leaps alive —
where death is! Alive!
He speaks truly who speaks the shade.

— Paul Celan (trans. Michael Hamburger)

X

There is a second distance
        in the distance. The two are distinct

and want to meet, but will never
        meet. When you go there you will come

to one and not the other like a body
        that hovers just beyond your form—

a mother you sense pulling away like a swarm
        of black bees from the hive, soft,

with the spring lethargy of a lover.
        Father is a future metric spacious enough

to outpace you. It is tiring to never really be
        fused to them, to never settle in the ballast

of treasure; tiring to fluctuate in a buzz
        that makes all space frantic, split.

Yet there you are in an old polaroid,
        held in the in-between. The three of you

reanimated by decay as a red wave
        moves slow but too soon eats furniture

then faces. Love's old postures appear
      like one long slouch

towards X — where X could be anything —
      a father, a mother, you, the stained couch.

Drift

One language for night
    another for day.

Therefore a fetus-wet
    fire in the brain

grants her the howl
    of boreal forests.

Therefore the father —
    an indelible moment
    that took her by surprise
    (a rodent's pink
        eyes.)

Fore of Father and
    Skin:
        (so-hum of only-
        ness: her/him)

Therefore to unknow his Herculean
    feet, his beard
        woven with clover.
        (only a god would do that)

        Circles he traces (yab––
        yum––)

over her crown: a skull,
    therefore,
        can open to the sky.

    (Can circle her back
        to the first therefore)

His potency

      is plural: (him/him)   What he gives her

         is contingency, feral instincts —

            but no language for loss or longing,

              no ode for father in retreat. His goneness
                 an everywhere, a quartzite and
                     karst she clings to
like a moon only he can name:
      (_____)

Therefore his love _____ / a boat she rows
      close to the glacier's split (death
        keeps leading the way)

Therefore the ice melt
      a stream from Mother's
        fevered head — wet, therefore,

    in the lap of a child.

        Therefore a child
           smooth as a whale bone

       plucked from the cliff
          in a town far from the sea.

Wing

We are not your   missing fathers
　　　　or children.   Our sudden red appearance

on a branch outside   your kitchen window
　　　　is not a sign   the melanoma

will subside. We are   not your personal
　　　　angels, prophets, spirit guides. We don't mediate

or transport prayers.   Hold no sway
　　　　with Other- or Outer-worlds.   We aren't ancient.

We guard no gates.   We aren't your higher selves.
　　　　Not your soul. Cut the shit: don't tell the kids

to try this; they will never really spread
　　　　their wings and   —

Stop calling it flight: we labor in the swarming
　　　　air, cerulean   burden, shifting thermals, dodge

the clench of talons. It's a living. Like the kiwi
　　　　emu, grebe, and Moa-Nalos,

Aukland Teal, Ascension Crake, Kakapo,
　　　　and the Inaccessible Island Rail,

we are plotting our escape   from the firmament.
　　　　Screw transcendence. While you aspire to aspire

we countervail: crave the bind of root, stasis
　　　　of iridium, weight of iron ore

un-dream ourselves into   the stolid
　　　　drag of the pedestrian.

Crash

No sun.
No sun with teeth.
No teeth or tongues on days you need.
Nothing to do or be.
I'm giving you this poem with nothing in it
in case you want the relief of the nothing it will give.
It works like a woman to give you that.
To not give you that.
There's music and some other noise, but that's not anything.
Maybe some crows hanging around with their rasps. Stentorian.
The hum of government is just the space
where something used to be. Inbox empty.
In the den, no fox. Matter, unsexed. Your body talks of pain
but it's phantom. Nothing in the cracks on your molars
but the suchness of a future. (Let's not go so far as dead,
since that may still feel like something.) Nothing in the synapse
but leaps. No beginning in the Big Bang. Nothing in cells
but how you spark around your body, lighting up your insides
at all hours like a sun with teeth, which is not a thing,
and therefore you're beginning to think this might actually be
something, but the poem with nothing in it has to seem
like it's giving if it's going to deliver on the nothing you need.
I'm giving you this poem with nothing in it like a tear
in the fabric, no sun with lips or arms to turn you
into a blue narcissus. No baby teeth disappeared
from under the pillow. No birds of death.
No new forms of surrender. Terrors stirred.
Not dreams where clumps of hair and teeth
come loose in your hands,
not the viper pit or coronal hole.
No one really knows into which category a dream falls.
Or if it's right to say the poem with the hail storm

really has a hail storm in it. (Crash, yes.)
You might be looking at your hands now,
thinking how empirical they seem,
how they hold all the thunder of your mothers.

Weapon

To grow into a woman is to grow thick
with truth — its weight, its objective
uselessness, its huge feet, its dick. Far above
sea level the men go on squawking
in the rarified air the way echoes
from the Big Bang still coo
as primordial gravity waves in outer space —
it's true — cosmic booms so small
we don't hear. The truth is we listen to
men more than we listen to outer space. That's on us.
Attuned to the cluster of teenaged white
boys, the explosive noise of all the unearned power they hoard —
we cross the street so their truth will not see
or touch us and think: *Shutup*. Keep our back-talk
in the dresser drawer, keep it low until what's in it lives
clean and beyond any man's reach. Until our inner
space is silent as a ponderous weapon. The truth is that elephants
hold funerals, caress the flesh and bones of their dead.
They travel long distances to do this, to stroke
with the trunk's tender finger, the flesh and bones
of their dead. Sweet beast — in truth, you rape
the white rhino, then kill it with your tusks,
and when the gentle savanna rains prick your skin,
you can't endure the pain, and sink into the river for relief.

Cave

Even at my most primitive
I can't be the sort of violent
I long to be, clubbing facts
for sustenance. What's savage
is the way I knife
through a house without
children. Shut the blinds
and wait all day for the basest
self to arrive. The basest
self is old, can carry the carcass
in her teeth. What else
could be out there at the end
of my days? An open channel that
won't stay open. A noology of no
thought, just the whir in the brain
that undoes the central
idea of the woman, inserts
itself, snaps a little
muscle. My mouth bloodied
by the scruff I haul. That idea
is the reigning heavyweight
champ of my day. Pow. Bam.
Right in the kisser. I can't say
without ventriloquizing
a baby or a man; and if I speak
the carcass will fall.

Target

I've stalled out at the dreamery
where flying has everything to do
with killing, where I can't unhook
from what I fail to know, how we slayed
the serpents in the cradle and muscled
through — the root
of violence coded in our limbs.
I want to hit the tarmac feeling
verified in my rage like the locals
who carry rods and guns along the Rio Chama's
clay banks, a place I visit just to make myself
strange. A woman there once aimed a pink pistol
at me. The pinkness in her hands like a big
piece of Bazooka gum. It filled me with a joy
so fleshy and lost, a little joke folded
in the candy. I can still feel her mark
on my temple, the throb of a time that won't
depart. I will arrive to my death only once,
in the time of all time. The kill approaches
like a rattler in the sand, a generous mother
who gathers behind my eyes. To be suspended
in it, to keep this anger in transit, as if anger
were my locus — locked and loaded, singular,
tinged with the taste of iron. I pass the time,
sort bullet casings like pills. A vulture
watches the road. Someday, these hands will surrender
to the homeland, but never to each other.

Blow

Dear Annihilator,

The damage here is stunning. The stilled harm.
And the wind — Black Sanctus, Descendant
of Conquistadors, Bride of Space. An almost
visible body rippling earth's millennial
stripage, her post-historical thrashing.
It must have been one bitch of a gale
that carried this mess of sand
thousands of miles, sculpted
in homage to Jupiter.
Would it kill you to write?

Dear Annihilator,

Please don't respond.
I'm here at the foot of Cerro Pedernal
practicing Descendentalism which makes me think
about our seminar in that windowless room
in the Physics Building, breathing rarified air,
arguing the politics of rescue.
If only you'd unsee me.

Dear Annihilator,

The brain takes on dust in the desert,
the pointlessness of eons. A postcard from *Española*,
heroin capital, USA. Consider this a missive
from Duende. No road to Rescue.

Dear Annihilator,

I am not myself, but a voice outside of,
a presence unaware of its power
to harm. The landscape makes
this laughable: what more
can I do to the mangled junipers
and red-dirt ruins, spires and varves
of sandstone, prehistory whittled to dust.
I might be awful, but I'm harmless.

Dear Annihilator,

I just wanted more —
There's real power in my desire
to rush into spaces I can't fathom.
You, a fathomless space.

Dear Annihilator,

I want to drag myself through arroyos.
No. I want you to drag me through arroyos.
By my hair. Like a kill. Like the deer in possession
of some crushing musculature.
To clench on impulse. Right here, from
the center. I know you know.
A want that marks a deeper want.

Dear Annihilator,

You were right: it was erosion I was after,
the kind that takes the friction of lifetimes,
a personal army of men equipped to kill off
the father once and for all.
He'll never die

Dear Annihilator,

The violence of childhood —
is that the frisson between us?
Tours of duty in the high desert
give old anger a place to roam,
a new scale. Anger tracks me.
I prickle at the word *pounce*.

Dear Annihilator,

I'm conspicuous in my human form,
capacious. I see you in the cacti,
shrugging at me like *what*?
My only true enemies.
I confuse myself with the wind,
with night's perpetual falling.

Dear Annihilator,

Dust funnels thrash the tumbleweeds.
Kicked forty feet high, they spin
like spaceships or latticework eggs,
whir a dream helix. The past rises up
like that funnel, conjures itself out of
prairie dog dens. It looks close to our future:
dusty, blood-tinged.

Dear Annihilator,

When will I hear from you?
Stupid to ask. To make someone wait
is the prerogative of power. I meant

none of it. Each next letter I send
is a fistful of sand thrown in the wind.
All this outer space. *Can't* is what my body
shapes to, the charge of gravity
without a planet. *Wait* is what
shapes me. You. An era called eolian,
an eon of no that settles in.

Joke

I had an aspiration for a perfect friendship
with the parish priest. He was you.

I climbed into your fine house and spread my legs
at the vestibule so you could come in.

What does this say about me
when I dream.

The problem is that my dreams are never
funny. I can't think while I laugh, and I can't

laugh while I dream. I never say, *I heard this great joke
last night while I was sleeping.*

It must be the thinking that destroys
what happened during the dreaming.

(Or is it the dream state
that obliterates thought?)

Only the dream knows
the punchline, often forgotten.

I should be able to say this to you during waking hours
without laughing, but as you can see, it's not possible:

When I think of you, I think of a mansion or
a church where sex is the way in.

Baby

1.
Language is experienced
as matter by the dreamer,

for example: corpse of your mother
as gyrating ball, bright gaseous star

rekindled in some post-life orb.
Exoplanet. Her swirl

flashes purple — streaks of lung,
femur, white heat,

link of vertebrae, a cloudy blue
eye. The force stems

from her breath — exhales
a trade wind. After a while, you sort of

get it: her body and spirit are mixed up
in a furious whir

that simultaneously explodes
from her mouth as it is sucked

back into it by her will.
Spirare, explains Dream Speak,

is three things at once:
to blow, to expire, to die.

2.
blood fur or is it snow chatter
waking won't wake
dream chew fat icing dream matter
what's the fatter? the dream is the
walker the flesh chunks
pillow should say the wake is the
dreaming stay where you are
the dream and the woman who comes
rattling a metal tray
a scalpel scalps to lay teeth
on the pillow the woman
with bone teeth and comes
and sculpts and while you sleep and
not and do you wake to slice
the fat from the fragment but
no still snow no pain
cake in my mouth

3.
It's psychic anarchy to give me
all the babies I never wanted, the spiritual

automaton of motherhood,. A baby boy
in my arms and from his head

a pattern of veinous red
cracks over the body. He's tropical fern,

dying coral reef, rivose.
The rash branches like a weave

under his parchment
skin. He will crumble, turn to dust, useless

soma. Laborless births
drop an army of children into my lap

without forceps or theatrics.
According to Dream Speak,

my platonic's untouched. I love them more
than you'd love a non-dream child.

One is kidnapped
in a green Buick — he will suffocate

on the hot vinyl. It happens sometimes.
Even now, my nipples ache for him.

This one sleeps in a metal bed, the sort
you'd find in war time hospital.

All my darlings lined up in rows —
not like newborns or soldiers,

but still, an infantry
to strangle or suckle.

4.
You could go to church with your mom like she asked,
        but you really want to have sex

with X. you hop in the shower with him, which is public.
        other people are doing it

so you start doing it too. then your mother shows up, naked,
        her breasts enormous, areolas

perfect crimson discs. you're worried X will compare
        your breasts to your mom's,

which are superior. *this is just weird. she's too into it.*
        you notice black hair on her

thighs, her arms, and the sides of her breasts,
        like a primate. Dream Speak:

Revolting, but a relief — now you don't have to rival her,
        but why would she dress up as your father?

5.
Lover sends emoji text: face with heart
eyes/ face with skull eyes/pine trees /swan.

Husband suspects something's up. Must keep
jilted lover quiet or he'll spill.

It was only a kill
in my head, but the lover sends proof: a pair

of small pants through the mail —
doll-size. The baby

has shat herself; someone unfastens her diaper —
mangled genitals, a hot mess.

In the midst of this, the tragedy of peek-a-boo
dawns on her for the first time.

6.
Your stylist shaves a circle then applies a cream
that burns a halo on your scalp.

She pushes the remaining hair down and says:
now press your head to the stove, make the red circles

match up. All of this seems wrong, but you don't want
to act paranoid, so you do it.

The blistering tissue
is cervical; the halo

a castration. You want to say it looks
raw, but instead you go:

"It's how all the stylish ladies are wearing it
these days," loud enough for the whole salon

to hear. The women tuck up

under their dryers; they could give a shit
about how you look

in your self-inflicted wounds.

7.
A baby in a gift box.
thanks.

Girl in pink knit cap, baptismal gown —
body sunken, lost in organdy

like an egg waits, shrinks:
I replace the lid, tie a string

around it and strap it
to the coffin: *there, there*, I say,

with a pat. Then:
no — tear the box open, blow

into her mouth until
she stirs. What keeps telling me

to *box up!* and *inflate!*

My box/*Buchse*: euphemism
for the place

where all my gifts
come and go.

8.
Sick to mix sex with infants but the dreamer is an imbecile,
a murderer, a perv.

Baby with the noodle-schlong waving it around. Flagellum.
Tentacle. A jerk with power.

It's wrong but I'm going to *hop on* because the dream-speak
keeps insisting I *hop on*.

Oh, the deepest wish, to spray like a man. But the hose makes
for bad sex — I'm riding the tip of it

which keeps me at a great distance from the infant,
like an astronaut tethered

to the mothership, bouncing off lunar dust.
Dream-speak says it's umbilical:

To be made whole, you have to be the fetus
with a fetus on the line

She

women dressing up like women in women's dressing rooms. women —
many women — multiply and divide, wave many woman limbs in many
mirrors. women's arms heavy with women's dresses stitched by women
in Bangladesh. women in silk got woman trouble, women cocooned in
distress. ha-ha women! women threading through women's wear. women
shedding skins — synthetic and mammalian, shrunken in fibers of micro.
women draped in naphthalene, milling polyester in chilly vuggs of stuff.
women joined to the muchness of the voluminous. women swimming
mammalian in seas of textless textile. sexless women humming around
pumps and slingbacks texting selfness. women buy one/ women get one.
women looking. women pointing. thirsty women without votes or water.
women without land rights or songs of acquisition. women rich as wom-
en. women in a hot woman mess. mega-mega-women. women dialing
up women on the women's hotline, yarning a mythomoteur of women.
women stitching a women's genus, threading the woman species through
no-woman's land. women charged up in electrostatic muchness, charging it
to charge cards, in charge of nothing, charged with the soft crime of being
women.

Catch

If the kiss
of a man whose fear
bears out

the river's force —
If his mouth and hands
work in service

to the body's
turbid mulling —
If he wants

whatever's
under —
to hook and possess

the violent,
tug them,
feel an other —

To be reeled in
from the rapids
is a sexual

assault, a rainbow
trout thrashing
the air.

Preeminence
is what he feels —
the pulse that comes

before anything's
emitted or said —
the thread

he follows, so fine
to the mouth's
fresh cut.

Cost

A Slovenian Marxist philosopher travels to the desert with a film crew
to obliterate pleasure. He sits in the dunes, sips a Coke

a close up of thick glass bottles the Khmer Rouge used to store its fascist
medicine in the form of expired cure. Ideology, he suggests, is a death

investment. His drink is getting warm, he says, excremental — and this
raises some questions: *What's the cost of his thirst? How much for the
        eternal?*

*For the cure? Should we buy it or steal? How long until poets are paid
by line, word, feel?* His point is that healthy people are full of shame,

their entrails panoramic in wheatgrass and flax, as the rest corrode
in the more of the less, in the very same fizzle of the dying galaxy that
        tickled

O'Hara's cilia just before the tire of the dune buggy crushed him, the *it*
rising in excess. Creatures of global markets, there's no way to do his death

guilt-free — an iamb or a breath owns shares in pain; your non-death
the finite space you take up, the pile of knowledge or cash you hoard

for some future pleasure. *What would you pay to be the woman who mouths
florescent orange tulips around the birches? How much for the screen rights*

to be alive, sipping a Coke in the warm Manhattan 4 o'clock light? —
for O'Hara's death to slip through your spiracles with his intelligent giddiness,

and leave you sick, mute, broke?

Drive

You know you're a poet
if driving a car in America

threatens your dialectical
reversals, the radical

autonomy of the highway
like a corpse who lays down

and dies a second time
just for you. The asphalt is classless

and hierarchical, an expanse
of carcasses — whitetails and possums,

lost dogs and turtles — all without
an "I" — for you. Every way opens

an anti-Marxist utopia: densest forests
part, rivers plunge underground. Tires

unpeel dioxins in atmospheres.
You don't deserve this. You drive

like a statue with no head, a cobra
with legs. Shiva's devoted nāgá

who won't cop to his own
religion, pursued in the frantic

speed of the mind's mind
which is always miles ahead

and miles behind. The bumpersticker
on the truck says: *How's My Dying,*

and you see the big poetic crash
waiting for you out there, the final

horizon on your woundedness.
In your fish-eye vision, creatures

of the forest perform honor suicides
with a thwump against your grill.

You feel it like a blow to your overgrown
cerebral cortex: even without ideology

the autonomous animals have done things
for you — unspeakable things

in the name of freedom.

Bind

If you meet the Buddha in the street,
        melt him down, cast
bullets. That's what Mao did —
        cast him into
densest sonnet form.
        You only think
you want emptiness
        because you are already
99.999996 percent
        empty. By existing
you are in tune
        with the empty
pulse of the empty
        universe. It's not necessary
to connect
        with what you mean,
the elusive reply you think
        your shrink's
waiting for. You'll never
        please her. Talking is as
pointless as chanting, which is as
        pointless as silence.   Dear child,
the resonant space that holds us
        together and pulls us
apart is what we are —
        blessings
and the obstruction
        to blessings.

Burn

Infants and accidents, long convalescents
who fail, failures who ripen

then fail, your neighbors, ancestors, who arrive
in steady procession by pickup, boxes slipped

onto gurneys, wheeled to the conveyor
where they glide like a fleet into the flames.

The retort door shuts and their bodies burn
for hours a night, sometimes longer.

At Morningside Crematory, a man unearths a corpse
or digs a grave. No, he masturbates over the mossy

stones of infants. He begs them to keep burning,
summons back their lives, uncommon as comets.

All around him, the furnace's shudder
leaks a bleary sheen. The ashes twirl, melt

on his tongue like hosts; oaks go watery
with death's green face. To feel the atoms

drift and disperse, cleave to other
bodies, brings a rush. His final shivers

like the trace of the dead looking
through: — heat of memory — a barrel fire

in autumn, his father brooding in his wool
cap as the embers of the *Evening Sun* ascend

through dusk. A child burrows nearby in a leaf pile.
Simmering, silent as ash, in the pulse

of finer particles where Whitman
could be right about the luck of death —

or whatever happens in the flash
of oriflamme and murl as we tip

into a fiery box of the mind.

Pin

It rains in hallways. You have a body part
called dorsal. A woman without gravitas

has gravitas. The concierge hands you
a slender indigo umbrella. A man who would never

paint his nails has painted his nails (red).
He wants to pin you (to something).

The woman with(out) gravitas is reciting
her poems. Someone whispers:

nail him. The poems are mediocre, thin,
but something about your wet fin makes us

listen. The walls are porous.
There's (no) love.

Swim

1.
Sickness of wet. Six glasses of father.
I'm swimming under the ocean with three
muscular lions. Who knew I'd be souling like this?
The Dream: loss and recall, things with alarms,
fangs, fur chilled or warmed. Wetness a
wantness. No sugar no sun. All sog.
Food rot in tanks and barrels. I'm swimming
without breathing, the lion's muscular
freestyle soul. Here's the dream maker
in the mirror. Here's my dream beer
that won't ferment. Sore with downpour.
Six glasses of mother. Nothing that won't drown.

2.
When the bear finally arrives, he's starving.
He wants whatever's in my little blue
basket, the Tupperware and the bronze
dildo that drove the emperor wild. The seals
are in cahoots, cheering from the waves, clapping
flippers. Outlaw of satisfaction, I forget
they eat flesh, mine if they can get it.
Carnivorous mouths of mist and vague;
I want the bear to grasp the dildo
to see how it behaves in his clutch;
to behold the bear beholding and not know
if it's a sandwich or a six shooter,
and when he discovers it is neither,
like me — to not be able to name that feeling.

3.
The bay at the end of the road
is not the edge of a nation or shelf, not
the little grass shadows that wave —
water the great come-on, lover
you want but can't hold. Knee deep
you beg — for the end or at least more sex
in the tide's suck. Ocean or pelvic floor,
your private basin, the lure of black laver
a longing that drops. Are you bottomless?
Pensivehead? Can't fulfill? Gripped to earth
as you are? What a gorgeous cape of regret
you wear, the tide fans out before you,
assertion of your hands — fingers as
ripple and drift — spread out before you.

4.
The women are complaining
about their hair, how they hate it.
They wish it freer, bluer,
more aggressive. The women
are falling to the floor in protest
of hair and the president,
taking up sheers and blade.
Now their skulls are an army
of stubble. Now their hair fills
his pillows. The president
tweets he *hates that*
calls them *so mean.*
Wake up, they tell him,
it's time to shave the worm.

5.
Rain through borders —
a fish twists in my chest.
Swims close spaces, skims
valves, ribs.
The fish knows why/how
to stay hidden; like the rain
it just won't quit.
I grow mossy with it.
Limbs drop, turn
to flourishes in hollows
unseen, the sweet shuffle
of platelets. The fish inside
won't be halted by staunch;
to swim, it must keep me bleeding.

6.
I love hate the beauty here, the lush
on lush crime, you know how wild
I am about trees their arms draped
in conjugations of green, wild arms
that hold nests of sickness.
I love hate my want to climb
into those arms, how it obsesses
like a baby bird, my mouth
gaped to a sap that licks me
back. Little trap; I lean into
redwoods for cure
cedars for radar —
they feed back the sickness,
a body scan of green.

7.
The furniture breaks under you
while you figure out what makes
blue blue. A grave settles seaward.
The dull birds have wants, a justice
that won't map on. It's the only music
they know, a you that's really an I.
The pulse and minus of a man
who permeates my skin. My veins
outbeaming in death practice.
A tongue to gag. It's all untrue.
Sleep is where I fear, and fear
never needs me to know a thing.
Like the cat, the soul can't decide:
it wants in, then out, then in again.

8.
In oyster piles you saw their boots,
men who'd made an art of it.
You crushed the shells and boiled them
into confused ink, wrote letters to sailors
lost at sea. *Mayday, mayday*, you said.
You wanted health care from trees,
education from oxygen. The air had
a bluster you couldn't trust.
You wanted a country of women
to breathe you out of this one.
The bay asked for your labor
but not too much. *Get to work*,
it said, and meant your work
should go undetected.

9.
Here you think in mist, not
foggy or mystical, but specific
talk from the cliffs. Yes,
they are moving, crevices in you,
five times a day cycle like prayer
until you see your hands, the way
they climb and mudra, less archetype
than water. Until you don't know
what water or your hands
could ever stand for. Not for their use,
value, clue. Not to dive the interior.
What you fall in, awash in a paralysis
of yes—a wreck that burns in you
like a forest of moss.

10.
She would kill something very small
first. An ant. Then eat it. She would think
about how that felt. How much it hurt
the ant; how much it hurt her.
Then she'd move on to newts, sparrows,
toads, even the little rabbits she loved, higher
forms with more capacity for pain.
She needed to know if she could slit
a pig's throat and still enjoy the pulled pork.
She wakes at 3 a.m. and stabs a whale in the neck.
It's not a dream. Her killing makes her famous.
She wins the prize for Non Performing
Person; next year she places second
for The Last Dead Thing.

11.
A lightening strike cracked; your mother
vanished in smoke. Now every charred
stump is her, every old growth
a woman you must fuck/kill/fell.
I'm trying to see, you say, your lens trained
on fog, whorls, spray. You study maps
of their vanishing. In another life,
you get drunk at night and punch
men who punch back. Men are good
like that. Mist is the one who asks too much —
to slip into sheets. She lifts you to her skin
makes the air big until everything breathes again —
moss and fern, the bright streak in the sky,
the giant trees, names forgotten, old as god.

12.
A bud plus a droplet. Both in silver
quaking. You watch even though
you know: tension builds, then
relents. An ancient stress.
To open or fall, no big thing.
Love or kill, come from/
vanish into. But here you stand
seen as you are, holding a little light,
a lot of blue. Suspect? Me too.
The way you square with your
resistance, cradle a clump of moss
in the crook of your neck. Like a trick
on softness. How you do all of this
like a man, until you don't.

13.
There is an eye that is everywhere for which
you have no name. A perpetual daughter like
the wind or lichen, whatever hangs
from these trees, the most seductive wisps.
On a fault line somewhere in Nevada, the feds
have buried their zombies. No one tells you
about such things, or that the ocean is mostly
disappointment, or who named the road
Starvation. Do you want to be a doctor? a lawyer?
Do you wake in the night and need to be fed?
I'm kidding when I tell these tales. The nukes
are safe in their cradles. The earth lulls them
to cathedrals. They will never wake hungry.
I will never be your mother.

Snake

1.
Dream Speak won't talk. Never
mentions the cash and the cancer,

the bacteria that carve
the chest in sleep. Infection scars.

From the right side — the righteous
side — skin pulls away

in soft clumps. The gash it leaves
is vaginal. A moray eel twists, anchors

a tooth in your flesh. Dream Speak says
don't worry, it's only an eel of mores.

Moray from morena: to be rich, to possess
authority. But was it cause or cure? Ancient

Greeks would lay the dreamer
on the stretched skin of a sacrificed ram,

rub her in oils — frankincense and myrrh,
make her quodesh, mostly holy, and watch over

until she dreamt her own cure.
But the mystics are extinct, no one left

to read the cryptic of skin's scarabs, this missive
of entrails. Every dreamer abandoned

to an excess of flesh — every dreamer
her own oracle and anointer.

2.
To diagnose, he sniffs
my nostrils, all my slits

and spiracles. *Dear Doctor,*
I didn't ask for this.

He hisses from his scaly head,
coils up my torso: *take a deep*

breath, he says. The verdict:
breath is fine, a little sour, red blood cells

too high in red. Doctor prescribes
a powder from the earth —

no plant, all mineral. *It's potatoes*
that drive the redness up,

and the green magnetic fields in Ireland
where you and they were grown.

3.
To think through the parasites in our guts
he must make an incision in our sides —

whoever does this next time will cut
the worms laterally, then glue them back

and leave them in our stomachs for exactly
sixty nights or we will die. The man and I escape,

but to what? Blue piping snakes from our abdomens,
looping from kidneys, transparent tubes coiled

around our arms like extension cords.
We think we must hide the source

of all this duct work, tuck the entrails
under ponchos. What will happen when our fluids

fill the lines? Dream Speak says: *You'll be very uncomfortable,
just as many in the world are forced to be very uncomfortable.*

From a rooftop we climb through a window
into a fetid, cramped flat where a group of Chinese women

crouch in fear. *Thank god*, I say to the women, *we're here*.
But the man is already on fire, sweating to death

from the worms still inside.

4.
In the Krishna or Mississippi —
the kind of deep rapids where you could buy it —

a nagini rises through the current,
a Vishnu bloom. Two plastic snakes

chase us — deadly, we know, by their bright coils
and the fact of their plasticness, segments

faceted, manufactured. I cut crescent strips
of genuine snake flesh — soft and white from the belly —

stitch them to my brow. *The central channel of the body
is a woman*, says Dream Speak. The snake flesh

a second set of eyes for the dreamer.
I turn to you and say: *where there's danger,*

I am the danger, and a water moccasin bites
my tongue. I spit froth. The paramedics

tell me to wait on the riverbank. Dream Speak says:
I wouldn't trust them, I think they're really parametrics.

5.
We're sexual jerks, oysters and little forks, babies and snakes.
      In the dream I'm dating R, I've known since we were eight.

We're babies and lawbreakers, jawbreakers and gum,
      sticky residue of. We make out in the movies while on screen

killer whales and dolphins go at it, and I put my head in his lap and part
      the shirt. We're big mammals, squid, amphibians, angels

that wrestle. I taste from his bosom-bone like Whitman said,
      his blood-salt, like a whale. We're sea creatures, star creatures,

dust and pollen. He's a fine black man, but the filmic light turns
      his skin white, and he's a felon. We're grotesque

and glowing sometimes, signaling in shadow into the projector's
      beam. We're the bullies and the bullied, the spoon bills

and the slips of lip. In the dream, R must leave me to fight
      with a knife. We're the target and the feathered arrow,

we're unnamed 'til now. *If you die*, I tell him, *it's my fault.*
      No, says R — We're the dream speak, the boss of nothing,

an American cinema that misreads your fin. Dream speak says:
      R for the rubbing you make of grave stones and men.

6.
The dog's head splits, each neck a plume
of mutual serpents.

Mutable. Beneficent and brutal,
he transubstantiates back to a dog,

compels us to look into the brown eyes
as we have evolved to do,

for clue, and there we recognize
the us and the not-us,

think of the worst, which causes him
to turn rabid again. Every time he finds

his wolf form, we conjure
the snake heads, cyclones

that howl. It's a game where we must
instruct ourselves

away from our urge for
evil. The longer we play,

the more primitive the beast,
the more sympathetic the breed.

7.
An old and noble *pensiero* to drive the giant snake from the family home,
        ritual waving of arms, shouting *Out, out!*

It falls on the eldest to chase him down the hall, shoo him
        from the foyer. Better to strangle it like an infant Heracles.

Outside, it's just more corridors, a game rigged by the snakes.
        Sometimes I glimpse his tail as he slips

around a corner, or lifts his body beyond the cornice, and my arms
        grow a little longer. This isn't about the absent father —

this isn't a wish to kill the numen who built this labyrinth,
        who couldn't love his own anatomy and architecture.

8.
To dine around a sunken table, smallest nibbles, poteen
sipped from mushroom caps.

We split a grapefruit wedge. I can't remember
which one he is. I search for an old notebook

where I have drawn all of them in pastel
with attributes, but the book is gone.

He's the red one, says Dream Speak, born clean
from mud, the one you meditate on as antidote

to desire. His locus in the human body
is the tongue. Should we share

a turtle bean? I ask. No, he says,
we've had our fill. I don't love him,

but the dinner of small portions
binds me to him like a consort.

Fold

That just-born hue of spring is post-
human, a color that does not belong
to systems of green or the holy —
meta-data of the new google eye.

You'd think the eye of a mind
would be more like an apple
blossom, but it's a fruit of non-
memory, residuals strewn like embers
from those tipsy dragons
in the crease who held us captive,
then set us free. Set free, you

stay put, stand at the window and praise
tulips, which appear as pixels
of an aftermath unaware of their
plasma potential — the spark
where all deaths get their start.

*

Dickinson shows up in the news crawler
to announce: a leaf is a disaster — it unfurls
from the navel of the hydrogen bomb,
possesses the sophistry of the tip jar.

Belief in our knowing lends cool distortion
to what we see. Mostly, we're oxygen
deprived. These are uneasy folds
for the modern woman to enter,
folds with no mathematical
cuts or platonic. To think the truth
was held in a crimp. Smoothed out

we may find ourselves at podiums
red faced, rubbing palms on our slacks —
knowledge spewers who quack
hermeneutic, hermeneutic — the false art
of reading for experience, like a duck
call brought too far out of the reeds.

Keep

A small voice like a rivulet told us what sex was and then another voice —
an article or a pamphlet — said the opposite. I only know ours
had something to do with the dog — his jowls, woof, paws —
and a softness that felt close and bottomless, that dwelt in the thud
of the heart's chambers like the sound of water when it plunges
to stone, hits a terminus, foams —

The sex was dark and bottomless like black water that rolls
under rapids and swells — a blackness arrested,
stilled rush, disappointing

if you expect the flat surface of sex, the sex of talk and touch.
We bark or growl because we don't believe in sex or god
but need it and him to believe in us —
a dog who gives freely and a god who withholds,
a pleasure that can't apprehend itself the way the dog doesn't know

what you mean when you say *I love you*, only a pitch that rises,
how his not knowing bears an honesty we can never approach,
as love received like the end's continuation, the water wall
beyond the rock, the thing that doesn't echo back.

Fin

Sweet, we know that heat
is not made up of many tiny
heats, but suns explode
with smaller suns. We know
travel is made from travail,
and the speed of wind increases
with height, built upon infinite
winds. If you listen to cell phone
conversations in airports, major fights
are comprised of hundreds
of thousands of bites
of perfectly true things.
You are composed of error (even though
you are perfect) and may feel a certain
distress, especially in a crowd, where you are
most vulnerable, most without me, most
likely to be falsified. Thank god
your new device has an app
that can map my luggage
as it moves through the prism
of the terminal. Thank god
you are there to channel
my lost motes (burden, hero,
cargo) from point to point.

It's lonely to travel towards you
so I turn to the man in the window
seat. He has a prosthetic hand
that scrapes the seat-back tray.
It seems too large and heavy, like a clump
of clay. Did he ever consider a super-powered
suction cup, or a hand of many hands?
What about a green knife, cut lily, a Pez dispenser
or a Taser? What about a mouth? Christ,

just think what joy a mouth-hand would bring!
Hi, he says into his device,
I'll call you when we land.

The flight is made up of minor,
tense moments that accumulate
to form one large tension
that expands to fill the space between
everyone on the plane until we all taste
a common gaseous disgust, like cotton
stuck to the roof of our mouths.
Fetid bodies locked in the fuselage,
panting, running low on life force, waiting
for a hero to make herself known.
To make the journey even more laborious,
I tell the flight attendant, I'll hang
a raw slab of meat around my neck.
I act this way to remind myself
something as small as a fin
separates me from you.

We have given over to the organizational
pull of the flight, and in this way we are
a function of too much plastic, sugar, and light.
Travel as torment, a metaphor none of us
understand. Metaphor a carrying over
we undertake, even though we don't know
we can bear it. Turbines reverse time. Texts
run between poles on humming wires.
Wings fly. I am here, at Gate A.
Call me when you land.

Buzz

Dear Alien, I want you
but can't read you

in the swelter of intel:
all this bug sex in the air, too

hot to rumble. Love
doesn't keep in the jungle,

hastens between ripe
and rot, the tropical version

of us is chaos and
chiasmus, a whatness in a forest

of whim that lurks in veils
of shadow and heat, a voodoo

that eats through paper,
wood, fruit and flesh

hastening between ripe
and rot. The giant toad stalks

the smaller toad,
as everything here is stalked

by the thing it is most
like and most counter to, the other set

of fangs snaking the gorge.

Dear Alien, the curse
sounds of decay: puck and pock,

  yawp of howlers in distant
branches calling tribe to tribe. The microbe's

  devouring intelligence knows
the sustenance of rot as I know

  the pull of your chest over mine —
equatorial. Open your teeth —

  so I can read you in
your green shirt, swinging the machete

  against a thousand shades
of green, beating back vines

  that tendril like my want,
by meters per hour.

  In the night, Dear Alien,
there must have been some quiet.

  Morning's softness blown open
by a crack: the sound of bodies

  breaking out — chicharra emerge
like angels in reverse, stumble into the light,

  clumsy-horny, whirring the obsessive
meta-chatter of some other talk

still held inside asteroids, siphoned
from the cells of stilt palms.

      To live in their buzz is excess —
a mesh beyond our range

      the wheeze of desire for
whatever is out there — the thing that tears

      the ether, breaks through
to the animal on the other side.

      The human ear only registers the *EEEEEE*
not the full thrum of their chambers

      feeding and breeding; a noise manufactured
in abdomens, piston-pumping muscles built

      for tympani. The air pixelates
with this sound. A slowed RPM track

      of their chatter pulses like a choir
of drugged cherubs. We nestle in,

      kin to the brood — gulp and rot,
gulp and rot.

      Once they were larvae who clung
to twigs, fell, pushed legs

through shells and burrowed
into the earth; a self-interment

before the becoming. You know best,
Dear Alien — you have to die first

then get born, then die again
to make yourself truly strange.

You have to be devoted
to the little tomb-bomb

of excrement and dirt
where you hunker for seventeen years

and dream the fast-lived
life. Cycles of seventeen for the oddness

and element of surprise, a prime
number to puzzle

whatever wants to eat you.
In seventeen years, birdish wisdom

fails, like ancient cures
or remorse for war.

What a racket — timbals,
chitinous membranes,

the ceaseless rubbing of legs
makes us frictional, Dear Alien, a little

confessional, the air too viscous
with sex, humid distances

revealed in waxy banana fronds.
Mauve flowers hang their blood-heavy

phalluses, a script that remains
exclusive between the bananas.

Dawn comes on again
like a dominatrix.

Their maumy bodies strewn
in the aftermath of a night's

frenzy toward the too-muchness.
They languish like nubile Greeks

on windowsills, cling to the screens —
we nudge them and they

shriek, erupt like jewelweed,
do a drunken bounce-hop

towards flight. The dead ones are left
to bullet ants who march in formation,

dismantle their limp, oversexed
corpses like an equatorial snuff film.

I would stay here with you, Alien,
until my heart regenerates, grows

    faithful, makes offerings to a less
benevolent god, the one who coaxes

    a waxy red flower to open itself
to another waxy red flower. Danger

    in mistaking an *etlingera elatior*
for an ecstasy that will last. Danger

    in the cataclysm of the bedroom's
opera, buzzed lovers ramming the screens,

    dying to get in and then
dying to get out.

    There is, after all, a purpose:
one hour of copulation

    produces six hundred eggs.
They mate for ten hours a day.

    Dearest Alien, do you think
deprivation leads to a fiercer

    attachment to this world?
Belief in a cause? What of the long

meditation underground? What do you know
of the stored up darkness?

Each one, isolated in its own
pod, somehow knows precisely

when the time comes— a knowledge
coded in the genome. Each one

in a brood of millions knows this,
all at once. All at once,

they dig to the near-surface,
carve a waiting cell, build a tiny

turret,
and wait again.

Did celestial bodies
in the rock that crashed to earth

become amino acids
in my body, and do they call

to your body and is that how
we know each other so poorly

and so well? You are alien and
familiar as the teeth of a skill saw

biting metal, a *whywhywhy*
rushing over me like an ancient poem

recited in the sips of xylem
siphoned through labia.

Their shimmy secretes a misty force field.
From tiny sphincters a bright elixir

showers down — a lingering elation,
a fugitive ode — pulp of palm,

temple of sound. I walk into it with you,
our bodies become glazed, gorgeous

and legible. Our skin shines like shook foil —
limbs like dewy aliens. To be writ

in the excretion of bugs is to be
the same, devoted to the decibels of some outrageous

plexus, cool as a wire brush
that skims the cosmic hi-hats.

Like insects, we drink deeply
until we are left stewing

in our own slew,
reduced to vats of sweat, spoiled

sugar, the biofuel of our future
child who will live to be

one hundred and fifty-five.
Broods of generations who came before

will pulse at her fingertips
in the finest data, and her face will bear

the patent of an acoustic literature,
sounding through eons' chambers.

How we pity all she'll need to know —
the wormholes she'll be asked to burrow,

hypertext of every vibration
ever made, all our wisdom no more

than a visage of winds that traverse
oceans and amass, but cannot die

or tell her the way, only give her
a map of a noise that accrues, a sound

that knows nothing
and means everything.

Sun again, my Alien. It drives me
wild, the feeling of my naked

body beaten by it — revved and
solar, my cells outbeaming

vying to suck the heat
from the host. My own hands

mad about my neck, my tongue
in love with my philtrum. What can I do

but burn out, then lull to the sense
I have climbed into a jungle and mistaken it

for womb; I have sucked
my own fingers, sticky with pleasure

have swooned to the just-born-
just-dead-just-sexed pulse.

There is more waiting than anything
else in this life, more lingering

in the buzz of perpetual nextness, yolked
as we are to some unknown future demand.

On cue we'll construct our own portal,
find a way out — and perform

for someone new. I want instructions
for the departure, Dear Alien, but in this life

no one can ever tell you
how it's done.

Thin

We oppose you, say the people, and vote yes
on Proposition Cull. The people's will

goes out into the air, and this the deer can smell.
They stomp and huff, kick loam. Hot mouthfuls

of breath taken up in the mist become
atmospheric, a new form of governance,

a future that hordes and loathes its own predation.
Once the deer were our mothers; now they seem

cynical, opportunistic, less terrestrial. More like us.
How blue the path where you are never alone,

in their eyes a primitive answer you want to un-know.
How blue is the green, green world, how it pulls

at your lungs. Give up your tongue,
the flash of white tail through the thicket, give up

your cud, your fawns, the little fox who trails you
sweetly to the stream. Let's retreat into the cave

and paint each other, cinematic in firelight
where our long kinship refuses to budge.

Civilly we aim for your heart. Step into our sights
where we fail to ID the enemy; give us the gentlest

thing in you that resists. Let's become pure
abstraction, taken into the bouquet of history,

swirl of spores, leafy post-thunder oils
that render us ions of ancestry.

Stay

To stay all night, to pass
the night as in prayer; to fail

the way the air often fails —
to be less light, more

qi. To strum in the manner
of atmospheres

traverse a sawdust
forest, a stream to harass

the janky spirit, a torrent —
to wait another year

for salmon to draw
their lovely quarrons

over quarrons, to be erratic,
raw in one's desire for

what's beyond the rapids.
To arouse a sense of

static; to cause to never
laugh again. To reside in

dissonance, chossy with root
juice and gristle. To be hurt

by flawlessness, measures of
success; to topple equilibrium,

cabbage a little cloth
from his coat in revenge.

   To mouth a dead language
at the edge of your city. To speak

   in the full faith of deadness.
To never come to the source.

   To make yourself prone
to small musics, sink

   your arm in loam, to touch
the spirit ditties of no tone.

Want

Whatever they want out there in the streets
the answer is no. No to the never forgetting.
No to the fat of yes.
No to the body's meridian, the tyranny
of health, the symmetry of death.

Whatever the pope is calling for,
no. No to the shamans divining a higher self.
No to machete, corpses unearthed.
No bullet, no background check.
No chokehold, no freedom.
No to the treaty, open hands of medicine men.

No to deathbirds, to winter and data,
human cargo lost at sea.
No to Whereabouts Unknown List.
No to the oil slick's rainbow, arabesques
left by shadow dogs pissing in snow.

No to the envelope of sleep, divine
intervention. To the sadhu who held his arm
overhead for thirty-two years and wants to lower it —
the arm simply says no.

No to Adam and the atom of yes, its storm
of no and no and no. We should have known
it would end up like this, a pack of slavering
mongrels chasing us into the impoverishment of no.

Yes we are practiced at poker faces, shake our heads
no-no/yes-yes, but no to ahimsa, to mothlight and Ginsberg,
his hipsterish angels who blathered on,
grew bitter, old, turned on their own,
robbed our sons and daughters of their no.

Notes

1.
A danger to enter from the sleep side —
a maze of grape vines on the slopes of Mount Vesuvius,
tarantellas rising from the Bay of Naples, from the dead
of the Herculaneum and Pompeii, embalmed in pumice and ash.
What arrives may be gargantuan, more than you can bear,
a giant baby waking in the gut of the volcano.

2.
There are two kinds of sleep, says Virgil — the Gate of Horn,
that offers *easy passage to all true shades*, and the Gate of Ivory,
radiant and flawless, but through which *the dead send us false dreams.*

3.
In the Temple of Isis, a painting
of the goddess greeting the horned Io, with a baby
at her feet like a house dog, and a snake in her lap
wrapped around her arm like a child.

4.
My dreams are fraudulent, identity thefts, bogus wounds,
spurious cures.
In *The Interpretation of Dreams*, Freud concludes:
>   *I think it is best, therefore, to acquit dreams.*

5.
House of Vettii, a fresco, 60-79 CE: the baby Hercules
strangles the snakes as his parents, Amphitryon and Alcmeene,
look on in shock. Heracles in Greek, meaning "glory to Hera,"
named for the goddess who sent the serpents to murder him
and his mortal twin in the cradle.

6.
The one who would kill us becomes our spiritual mother.

7.
Dream Speak says: *danger in naming your personal*
myth in this ancient maze. Fathers are babies; mothers
are snakes; there's an asp in the thicket — now what?
      (Now the shadow stalks its body.)

8.
What comes from us is often not of us: a flame and the smoke
rises, more powerful than the self. Dreams, said Freud,
are not absurd; they do not imply that one portion of our store of ideas
is asleep while another portion is beginning to wake. On the contrary,
they are psychical phenomena of complete validity... constructed
by a highly complicated activity of the mind.

9.
I was born in the borough of Clarks Summit,
Pennsylvania, as any child might be born — through the gates
of horn, helpless and monstrous, loved and reviled —tossed
in the crib to tussle with the increate real, to strangle and swallow
and succumb, to reshuffle the origin story. I was a miner
punching through earth, covered in silica.

10.
Myths drift. In the ruins of Pompeii, time
warped in the way of shades, my body
felt mythic, not like a city ruined, but one
perpetually emergent, dreaming an exit.

11.
The snake's infinity, the zeros and ones, were sent
by the gods or parents or teachers to destroy or falsify,

like a math problem that can only resolve itself
in more mystery. (Fathers: see: *Hercules*.
Mothers: see: *Hera*.)

12.
The earliest known image of the infant Hercules
strangling the snakes in his cradle is dated
around 480 B.C. Pindar writes about it in the *Nemean Odes*.
The scene was reproduced on coins and frescos.
vases and sculptures, and the Romans adorned their homes
and gardens with it, a domestic token of the more powerful
desires that rule us, the myths we still abuse.

13.
Dreams leak. They wrestle demons
and the divine, attempt to form the unformed
in a mixed mythology of Yahweh and Zeus — sinister
and innocent, quotidian and mystical, opposed
or associated, allied or estranged. Somewhere in these vines,
a young couple is wed, and the volcano's baby grows
restless, its violence wants to be fed.

14.
Snakes are child's play, child's play is seduction,
the work of the unconscious shadow boxing
with an irrational, cosmically mysterious thing.
As I kid, I pried boulders in the woods, scoured the chinks
of granite ledges, hunting snakes. I held them in my arms
like pets, let them slip down my shirt, up my pantlegs.
The trick was to hold still, to let the daimonic shiver
over your flesh, a thrill past fear, then
a private contentment —

Jules Gibbs

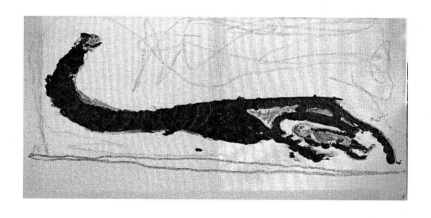